EMMANUEL JOSEPH

Wealth of Nations Reimagined, How Billionaires Are Rewriting the Rules of Power

Copyright © 2025 by Emmanuel Joseph

All rights reserved. No part of this publication may be reproduced, stored or transmitted in any form or by any means, electronic, mechanical, photocopying, recording, scanning, or otherwise without written permission from the publisher. It is illegal to copy this book, post it to a website, or distribute it by any other means without permission.

First edition

This book was professionally typeset on Reedsy.
Find out more at reedsy.com

Contents

1	Chapter 1: The Rise of the New Titans	1
2	Chapter 2: The Tech Revolution and Its Architects	3
3	Chapter 3: Global Influence and Geopolitical Power	5
4	Chapter 4: The Power of Philanthropy	7
5	Chapter 5: The Innovation Ecosystem	9
6	Chapter 6: Disruption and Creative Destruction	11
7	Chapter 7: Social Media Moguls and the Information Age	13
8	Chapter 8: The Future of Work and Automation	15
9	Chapter 9: The Climate Crisis and Sustainable Solutions	17
10	Chapter 10: The Influence of Media Moguls	19
11	Chapter 11: The Impact of Artificial Intelligence	21
12	Chapter 12: The Role of Billionaire Activism	23
13	Chapter 13: The Business of Space Exploration	25
14	Chapter 14: The Digital Economy and E-Commerce	27
15	Chapter 15: The Influence of Billionaire Sports Owners	29
16	Chapter 16: The Intersection of Wealth and Politics	31
17	Chapter 17: The Future of Billionaire Influence	33

1

Chapter 1: The Rise of the New Titans

In recent decades, the world has witnessed the unprecedented rise of billionaires who wield power far beyond their financial wealth. These new titans of industry have not only amassed vast fortunes but have also redefined the very concept of wealth and power. From the tech moguls of Silicon Valley to the influential investors of Wall Street, these individuals have reshaped industries, disrupted traditional economic models, and established themselves as key players on the global stage.

Elon Musk, the enigmatic founder of SpaceX and Tesla, epitomizes this new breed of billionaires. His ambitious vision of colonizing Mars and revolutionizing transportation has captured the imagination of people worldwide. Musk's journey from a young entrepreneur in South Africa to a global icon of innovation highlights the power of visionary thinking and relentless pursuit of goals. His ability to harness technology and leverage his influence has enabled him to achieve feats once thought impossible.

Similarly, Jeff Bezos, the founder of Amazon, has transformed the way we shop, read, and even consume entertainment. Bezos's relentless focus on customer satisfaction and his willingness to take risks have propelled Amazon from an online bookstore to a global e-commerce giant. His acquisition of The Washington Post and his foray into space exploration with Blue Origin further demonstrate his far-reaching ambitions and influence. Bezos's story underscores the transformative power of innovation and the ability to disrupt traditional industries.

These modern titans have also shown a remarkable ability to adapt and evolve in the face of changing circumstances. For instance, Mark Zuckerberg, the co-founder of Facebook, navigated the company through numerous controversies and challenges while continuing to expand its influence. Zuckerberg's ability to understand and shape social media trends has cemented Facebook's position as a dominant force in the digital age. His story exemplifies the resilience and adaptability required to thrive in an ever-changing landscape.

As we delve deeper into the world of these new titans, we will explore the factors that have enabled them to rise to such heights and the implications of their newfound power. From the role of technology and innovation to the impact of globalization and geopolitical dynamics, we will examine the forces that have shaped this new era of billionaire dominance. In doing so, we will gain a deeper understanding of how these individuals are rewriting the rules of power and reshaping the world we live in.

2

Chapter 2: The Tech Revolution and Its Architects

The advent of the digital age has been a game-changer, and the architects of the tech revolution have emerged as some of the most powerful individuals on the planet. The rapid advancement of technology has not only transformed industries but has also redefined the way we live, work, and communicate. At the forefront of this revolution are visionary leaders who have leveraged their expertise and ambition to build empires that shape the modern world.

Steve Jobs, the co-founder of Apple, is a prime example of a tech visionary whose impact continues to be felt long after his passing. Jobs's ability to blend creativity with cutting-edge technology led to the creation of iconic products like the iPhone, iPad, and MacBook. His relentless pursuit of innovation and perfection set a new standard for consumer electronics, making Apple one of the most valuable companies in the world. Jobs's legacy is a testament to the transformative power of visionary leadership in the tech industry.

Larry Page and Sergey Brin, the co-founders of Google, have also played a pivotal role in shaping the digital landscape. Their search engine revolutionized the way people access information, making the vast resources of the internet easily accessible to billions of users worldwide. Google's relentless focus on innovation and its ability to anticipate and adapt to changing trends have enabled it to remain at the forefront of the tech industry. Page and Brin's journey from Stanford University to building one of the most influential companies in the world underscores the importance of vision and persistence in achieving success.

Another prominent figure in the tech revolution is Satya Nadella, the CEO of Microsoft. Under his leadership, Microsoft has undergone a significant transformation, shifting its focus from traditional software to cloud computing and artificial intelligence. Nadella's emphasis on empathy, collaboration, and innovation has revitalized the company and positioned it as a leader in the tech industry. His story highlights the importance of adaptability and forward-thinking in navigating the ever-evolving tech landscape.

These architects of the tech revolution have not only created groundbreaking products and services but have also fundamentally changed the way we interact with technology. Their influence extends beyond the confines of their respective companies, shaping the broader tech ecosystem and driving progress in fields such as artificial intelligence, virtual reality, and renewable energy. As we explore the journeys of these visionary leaders, we gain a deeper understanding of the transformative power of technology and the individuals who have harnessed it to reshape our world.

3

Chapter 3: Global Influence and Geopolitical Power

In the contemporary world, billionaires have become major players on the global stage, wielding significant geopolitical influence. They are no longer confined to their boardrooms and businesses; their actions reverberate across nations and impact global politics. These individuals, through their wealth and strategic investments, have the power to shape public policy, support causes they believe in, and even influence election outcomes.

Take George Soros, for example, whose Open Society Foundations have been instrumental in promoting democratic values and human rights worldwide. Soros's philanthropic efforts and his active involvement in political affairs have made him a prominent figure in global geopolitics. His strategic donations and advocacy for progressive causes have both earned him praise and sparked controversy. Soros's story highlights the complexities and ethical dilemmas associated with wielding such immense power.

Mark Zuckerberg, the co-founder of Facebook, has also leveraged his platform's global reach to influence political and social landscapes. Facebook's role in shaping public opinion and its impact on elections have raised critical questions about the responsibilities of tech giants. Zuckerberg's actions and decisions have far-reaching consequences, demonstrating how billionaires can influence global affairs beyond their financial contributions. This chapter delves into the ethical considerations and challenges that arise from such concentrated power.

As we examine the global influence of billionaires, it becomes evident that their actions are often driven by a mix of personal convictions and strategic interests. Some, like Bill Gates, focus on global health and poverty alleviation through initiatives like the Bill & Melinda Gates Foundation. Gates's efforts to combat diseases such as malaria and polio have saved millions of lives and transformed communities. His story underscores the potential for positive change when immense resources are directed towards humanitarian causes.

However, the involvement of billionaires in global affairs also raises concerns about accountability and transparency. The concentration of power in the hands of a few individuals can lead to conflicts of interest and ethical dilemmas. This chapter critically examines these issues, highlighting the need for greater scrutiny and regulation to ensure that billionaire influence aligns with broader societal interests. As we navigate the complex interplay between wealth and power, we gain a deeper understanding of how these individuals are reshaping the global landscape.

4

Chapter 4: The Power of Philanthropy

Philanthropy has emerged as a key avenue through which billionaires exert their influence and leave a lasting legacy. Motivated by a desire to give back to society, many of the world's wealthiest individuals have pledged vast portions of their fortunes to charitable causes. This chapter explores the motivations behind their philanthropic endeavors and the impact of their contributions on society.

Bill and Melinda Gates, through their foundation, have become leading figures in global philanthropy. Their commitment to improving health, education, and economic opportunities for the world's most vulnerable populations has had a profound impact. The Gates Foundation's initiatives in vaccine distribution, agricultural development, and educational reform have transformed communities and saved countless lives. Their story exemplifies the potential for positive change when wealth is directed towards addressing pressing global challenges.

Warren Buffett, another prominent philanthropist, has pledged the majority of his fortune to charitable causes. His decision to donate his wealth through the Gates Foundation and other organizations reflects his belief in the power of philanthropy to effect meaningful change. Buffett's approach to giving, characterized by humility and pragmatism, serves as an inspiration for others in positions of wealth and influence. His story highlights the importance of thoughtful and strategic philanthropy in making a lasting impact.

However, the concentration of philanthropic power in the hands of a few individuals also raises important questions about accountability and representation. Critics argue that billionaire philanthropists, despite their good intentions, may inadvertently perpetuate existing power dynamics and inequalities. The chapter critically examines these concerns, exploring the potential risks and benefits of concentrated philanthropic efforts.

As we delve into the world of billionaire philanthropy, we gain insights into the complex interplay between wealth, power, and social impact. This chapter underscores the importance of transparency, accountability, and inclusivity in philanthropic endeavors. By examining the motivations, successes, and challenges of billionaire philanthropists, we gain a deeper understanding of how their actions shape the world and inspire future generations.

5

Chapter 5: The Innovation Ecosystem

The innovation ecosystem is a dynamic network of interconnected entities that drive technological advancement and economic growth. Billionaires play a pivotal role in this ecosystem, providing the capital, mentorship, and vision necessary to turn groundbreaking ideas into reality. This chapter delves into the various components of the innovation ecosystem and the ways in which billionaires contribute to its development.

Venture capital is a critical component of the innovation ecosystem, and many billionaires have made significant investments in promising startups. Figures like Peter Thiel and Reid Hoffman have not only provided financial support but have also shared their expertise and networks with budding entrepreneurs. Their investments in companies such as PayPal, LinkedIn, and SpaceX have not only yielded substantial returns but have also fostered innovation and economic growth. This chapter explores the symbiotic relationship between billionaires and startups, highlighting the mutual benefits and transformative potential of their collaboration.

In addition to venture capital, research and development (R&D) play a crucial role in driving innovation. Billionaires often fund R&D initiatives, either through their own companies or philanthropic organizations. For example, Larry Ellison, the co-founder of Oracle, has invested heavily in medical research through his foundation. His support for cutting-edge research in areas such as cancer treatment and aging has the potential to yield groundbreaking discoveries. This chapter examines the impact of billionaire-funded R&D on technological advancement and the broader implications for society.

Another key aspect of the innovation ecosystem is the role of education and talent development. Many billionaires have established or funded educational institutions and programs to nurture the next generation of innovators. For instance, Michael Bloomberg has made substantial contributions to higher education, supporting institutions such as Johns Hopkins University and Bloomberg Philanthropies' educational initiatives. By investing in education, billionaires help cultivate a pipeline of skilled talent that drives future innovation. This chapter discusses the importance of education and talent development in sustaining the innovation ecosystem.

The innovation ecosystem is also characterized by collaboration and partnerships. Billionaires often collaborate with other stakeholders, including governments, non-profits, and research institutions, to address complex global challenges. For example, the Breakthrough Energy Coalition, founded by Bill Gates and other billionaires, aims to accelerate clean energy innovation through collaborative efforts. This chapter explores the power of partnerships and the collective impact of collaborative initiatives in driving progress and innovation.

6

Chapter 6: Disruption and Creative Destruction

Disruption and creative destruction are fundamental principles of economic progress, and billionaires are often at the forefront of these transformative processes. By challenging established industries and introducing innovative solutions, they drive economic growth and reshape markets. This chapter examines the concept of disruption and the ways in which billionaires have harnessed it to create new opportunities and redefine the status quo.

One of the most notable examples of disruption is the rise of ride-sharing companies like Uber and Lyft. Travis Kalanick, the co-founder of Uber, revolutionized the transportation industry by offering an alternative to traditional taxi services. Uber's rapid expansion and success not only disrupted the taxi industry but also paved the way for other gig economy platforms. Kalanick's story highlights the potential for disruptive innovation to create new markets and redefine consumer behavior.

In the retail sector, Jeff Bezos's Amazon has been a disruptive force, transforming the way people shop and consume products. Amazon's emphasis on convenience, competitive pricing, and vast product selection has challenged traditional brick-and-mortar retailers and reshaped the retail landscape. Bezos's relentless focus on innovation and customer satisfaction has driven Amazon's success and cemented its position as a dominant player in the e-commerce industry. This chapter explores the impact of Amazon's disruption on the retail sector and the broader implications for consumer behavior and market dynamics.

The financial industry has also experienced significant disruption, with fintech companies challenging traditional banking and financial services. Billionaires like Elon Musk have been at the forefront of this disruption, with companies such as PayPal revolutionizing online payments and digital transactions. Musk's vision of a cashless society and his innovative approach to financial technology have driven the adoption of digital payment solutions and reshaped the financial landscape. This chapter delves into the impact of fintech disruption and the transformative potential of digital finance.

Disruption is not without its challenges and controversies. The process of creative destruction often leads to job displacement, regulatory hurdles, and societal resistance. This chapter critically examines the implications of disruption, highlighting the need for thoughtful regulation and responsible innovation. By understanding the complexities and nuances of disruption, we gain insights into the ways in which billionaires drive economic progress and the challenges that arise from their transformative efforts.

7

Chapter 7: Social Media Moguls and the Information Age

The rise of social media has revolutionized the way we communicate and consume information. Billionaires who have built empires in this space wield significant influence over public discourse and societal trends. This chapter explores the impact of social media moguls on the information age and the ways in which they have reshaped the media landscape.

Mark Zuckerberg, the co-founder of Facebook, has been a central figure in the social media revolution. Facebook's vast user base and its role in connecting people worldwide have made it a powerful platform for communication and information sharing. Zuckerberg's ability to understand and anticipate social media trends has driven Facebook's success, but it has also raised critical questions about privacy, misinformation, and the ethical responsibilities of social media platforms. This chapter delves into the challenges and controversies surrounding Facebook and its impact on society.

Jack Dorsey, the co-founder of Twitter, has also played a significant role in shaping the social media landscape. Twitter's real-time nature and its ability to amplify voices have made it a key platform for political discourse, social movements, and public debates. Dorsey's vision of an open and transparent communication platform has both empowered individuals and posed challenges in terms of content moderation and the spread of misinformation. This chapter examines the influence of Twitter on public discourse and the ethical considerations that arise from its use.

Other social media platforms, such as Instagram and TikTok, have also emerged as influential players in the information age. Billionaires like Kevin Systrom and Zhang Yiming have leveraged their platforms to shape cultural trends and drive consumer behavior. The visual-centric nature of Instagram and the short-form video format of TikTok have resonated with younger audiences, creating new opportunities for content creators and influencers. This chapter explores the impact of these platforms on the media landscape and the ways in which they have redefined content consumption.

As we navigate the complexities of the information age, it becomes evident that social media moguls have a profound impact on the way we perceive and interact with the world. Their platforms have democratized access to information and empowered individuals to share their voices, but they have also introduced new challenges and ethical dilemmas. This chapter critically examines the role of social media moguls in shaping the information age and the broader implications for society.

8

Chapter 8: The Future of Work and Automation

The future of work is undergoing a profound transformation, driven by advancements in automation and artificial intelligence. Billionaires at the forefront of these technologies are shaping the future of work, redefining job roles, and influencing labor markets. This chapter explores the impact of automation on the workforce and the ways in which billionaires are driving this transformation.

Elon Musk's ventures, including Tesla and SpaceX, are prime examples of how automation is reshaping industries. Tesla's use of robotics and AI in manufacturing has revolutionized the automotive industry, leading to increased efficiency and productivity. Similarly, SpaceX's advancements in rocket technology and autonomous systems have redefined space exploration. Musk's vision of a future driven by automation and AI underscores the potential for technological advancements to transform traditional industries and create new opportunities.

Another key figure in the automation revolution is Jeff Bezos, whose company Amazon has pioneered the use of robotics and AI in logistics and fulfillment centers. Amazon's extensive use of automation has streamlined operations, reduced costs, and improved delivery times. However, it has also raised concerns about job displacement and the future of work for human employees. This chapter examines the impact of Amazon's automation efforts on the workforce and the broader implications for the labor market.

Bill Gates, through his philanthropic initiatives, has also addressed the future of work and the challenges posed by automation. The Gates Foundation's focus on education and workforce development aims to equip individuals with the skills needed to thrive in an automated world. Gates's efforts to promote lifelong learning and reskilling highlight the importance of preparing the workforce for the changing nature of work. This chapter explores the role of education and training in mitigating the impact of automation on employment.

As we look to the future, it becomes clear that automation and AI will continue to shape the world of work. Billionaires driving these technological advancements have a significant influence on the direction of labor markets and the opportunities available to workers. This chapter critically examines the benefits and challenges of automation, highlighting the need for thoughtful policies and strategies to ensure a balanced and inclusive future of work.

9

Chapter 9: The Climate Crisis and Sustainable Solutions

The climate crisis is one of the most pressing challenges of our time, and billionaires are playing a crucial role in addressing it. Through innovative technologies, strategic investments, and philanthropic efforts, these individuals are driving sustainable solutions and advocating for environmental stewardship. This chapter explores the ways in which billionaires are tackling the climate crisis and the impact of their initiatives on global sustainability.

Elon Musk's commitment to sustainability is evident in his ventures such as Tesla and SolarCity. Tesla's electric vehicles and energy storage solutions have revolutionized the automotive industry, reducing carbon emissions and promoting renewable energy. SolarCity's solar power systems have made clean energy more accessible to consumers. Musk's vision of a sustainable future and his efforts to combat climate change underscore the potential for innovation to drive environmental progress.

Jeff Bezos, through his Bezos Earth Fund, has pledged significant resources to address climate change and protect the natural world. The fund supports initiatives focused on conservation, renewable energy, and sustainable agriculture. Bezos's commitment to environmental causes highlights the importance of philanthropy in driving climate action and supporting projects that aim to mitigate the impacts of climate change. This chapter examines the impact of the Bezos Earth Fund and other philanthropic efforts on global sustainability.

Bill Gates, through Breakthrough Energy, has also been a prominent advocate for climate action. Breakthrough Energy supports the development of innovative technologies that aim to reduce greenhouse gas emissions and promote clean energy solutions. Gates's focus on sustainable development and his efforts to foster collaboration among scientists, entrepreneurs, and policymakers highlight the importance of collective action in addressing the climate crisis. This chapter explores the role of technological innovation and collaborative efforts in driving sustainable solutions.

The involvement of billionaires in climate action also raises important questions about accountability and the influence of private wealth on environmental policy. This chapter critically examines these issues, highlighting the need for transparent and inclusive approaches to climate action. By understanding the contributions and challenges of billionaire-driven initiatives, we gain insights into the ways in which these individuals are shaping the future of sustainability and the broader implications for global environmental stewardship.

10

Chapter 10: The Influence of Media Moguls

Media moguls have long wielded significant influence over public opinion and cultural trends. In the digital age, their power has only grown, as they control vast networks of information and entertainment. This chapter explores the role of media moguls in shaping public discourse and the ways in which they have adapted to the changing media landscape.

Rupert Murdoch, the founder of News Corporation, is one of the most influential media moguls in history. His media empire includes major news outlets such as The Wall Street Journal, The Times, and Fox News. Murdoch's ability to shape public opinion and influence political outcomes has made him a controversial figure. His story highlights the power of media ownership and the impact of media moguls on society.

In the digital era, new media moguls have emerged, leveraging technology to build media empires. Jeff Bezos's acquisition of The Washington Post is a prime example of this trend. Under Bezos's ownership, The Washington Post has embraced digital innovation and expanded its reach, becoming a leading source of news and analysis. Bezos's influence on the media landscape underscores the evolving role of tech billionaires in the world of journalism.

Reed Hastings, the co-founder of Netflix, has also revolutionized the media industry with his streaming platform. Netflix's original content and global reach have transformed the way people consume entertainment. Hastings's vision of on-demand, subscription-based entertainment has disrupted traditional media models and reshaped the entertainment industry. This chapter examines the impact of Netflix and other streaming platforms on media consumption and cultural trends.

As we explore the influence of media moguls, it becomes clear that their control over information and entertainment has far-reaching implications. The concentration of media ownership raises critical questions about diversity, objectivity, and accountability. This chapter critically examines the role of media moguls in shaping public discourse and the ethical considerations that arise from their influence.

11

Chapter 11: The Impact of Artificial Intelligence

Artificial intelligence (AI) is poised to revolutionize various aspects of our lives, and billionaires are at the forefront of this technological wave. Their investments in AI research and development are driving advancements that have the potential to transform industries and improve society. This chapter explores the impact of AI and the ways in which billionaires are shaping its future.

Elon Musk's OpenAI initiative aims to ensure that artificial intelligence benefits all of humanity. OpenAI's research focuses on developing safe and ethical AI technologies that can address global challenges. Musk's commitment to AI safety and his advocacy for responsible AI development highlight the importance of ethical considerations in advancing this powerful technology. This chapter delves into the potential of AI to drive progress and the need for safeguards to prevent unintended consequences.

Sundar Pichai, the CEO of Google and Alphabet, has also been a key player in AI development. Under his leadership, Google has made significant strides in AI, with applications ranging from natural language processing to autonomous vehicles. Pichai's vision of AI as a tool to enhance human capabilities and address societal challenges underscores the transformative potential of this technology. This chapter examines the impact of Google's

AI initiatives and the broader implications for various industries.

Bill Gates's involvement in AI through initiatives like the Gates Foundation and Microsoft highlights the potential of AI to address global health and education challenges. AI-powered solutions in healthcare, such as diagnostic tools and personalized treatment plans, have the potential to improve patient outcomes and reduce healthcare costs. Gates's focus on leveraging AI for social good underscores the importance of using technology to address pressing global issues. This chapter explores the potential of AI to drive positive change and the ethical considerations that arise from its development and deployment.

As we look to the future, it becomes evident that AI will play a central role in shaping our world. Billionaires driving AI research and development have a significant influence on the direction of this technology and its impact on society. This chapter critically examines the benefits and challenges of AI, highlighting the need for responsible and ethical AI development to ensure that its potential is realized for the greater good.

12

Chapter 12: The Role of Billionaire Activism

Billionaire activism has become an increasingly prominent force in addressing social and political issues. Through their wealth and influence, billionaires advocate for causes they believe in and drive change on a global scale. This chapter explores the role of billionaire activism and the impact of their efforts on society.

George Soros's Open Society Foundations have been at the forefront of promoting democratic values, human rights, and social justice. Soros's activism spans a wide range of issues, from supporting civil society organizations to advocating for criminal justice reform. His strategic use of philanthropy and advocacy has made a significant impact on global social and political landscapes. This chapter examines the influence of Soros's activism and the ethical considerations that arise from his involvement in political affairs.

Tom Steyer, a billionaire investor and environmental activist, has dedicated significant resources to combating climate change and advocating for sustainable policies. Through his organization, NextGen America, Steyer has mobilized young voters and supported progressive candidates committed to environmental and social justice. His activism highlights the power of wealth in driving political change and addressing pressing global issues. This chapter explores the impact of Steyer's activism and the broader implications for environmental advocacy.

Laurene Powell Jobs, through her Emerson Collective, has focused on education reform, immigration, and social justice. Her holistic approach to philanthropy and activism aims to address systemic issues and create lasting change. Powell Jobs's efforts to promote equality and opportunity underscore the potential for billionaire activism to drive progress in critical areas. This chapter examines the influence of her activism and the challenges associated with addressing complex social issues.

As we explore the role of billionaire activism, it becomes clear that their efforts can have a profound impact on society. However, the concentration of power and influence in the hands of a few individuals also raises important questions about accountability and representation. This chapter critically examines the benefits and challenges of billionaire activism, highlighting the need for transparent and inclusive approaches to social and political advocacy.

13

Chapter 13: The Business of Space Exploration

Space exploration, once the domain of government agencies, has increasingly become a field dominated by private enterprises led by visionary billionaires. Their ambitious projects are pushing the boundaries of human achievement and opening up new frontiers. This chapter explores the role of billionaires in the business of space exploration and the impact of their endeavors on the future of humanity.

Elon Musk's SpaceX has been at the forefront of the private space race, with groundbreaking achievements such as the first privately-funded spacecraft to reach orbit and the development of reusable rockets. Musk's vision of making humanity a multiplanetary species and colonizing Mars has captured the imagination of people worldwide. His relentless pursuit of this goal and SpaceX's remarkable achievements underscore the transformative potential of private space exploration.

Jeff Bezos's Blue Origin is another major player in the field of space exploration. With a focus on building a future where millions of people live and work in space, Blue Origin is developing advanced rocket technology and space infrastructure. Bezos's commitment to space exploration and his long-term vision for humanity's presence beyond Earth highlight the importance of private investment in advancing space technology. This chapter examines the impact of Blue Origin's initiatives on the space industry and the broader implications for human space exploration.

Richard Branson's Virgin Galactic has also made significant strides in the realm of commercial space travel. By offering suborbital spaceflights to private individuals, Virgin Galactic aims to make space tourism a reality. Branson's vision of democratizing space travel and his efforts to create a new market for space tourism underscore the potential for private enterprises to drive innovation in space exploration. This chapter explores the impact of Virgin Galactic on the space tourism industry and the broader implications for the commercialization of space.

As we delve into the business of space exploration, it becomes clear that billionaires are playing a crucial role in pushing the boundaries of human achievement. Their ambitious projects and substantial investments are driving technological advancements and opening up new possibilities for humanity. This chapter critically examines the benefits and challenges of private space exploration, highlighting the need for international collaboration and responsible stewardship of space resources.

14

Chapter 14: The Digital Economy and E-Commerce

The digital economy and e-commerce have transformed the way we conduct business and interact with the marketplace. Billionaires who have built empires in this space wield significant influence over global commerce and consumer behavior. This chapter explores the impact of the digital economy and e-commerce on the business landscape and the ways in which billionaires are shaping its future.

Jeff Bezos's Amazon has been a driving force behind the growth of e-commerce, revolutionizing the way people shop and consume products. Amazon's emphasis on convenience, competitive pricing, and vast product selection has challenged traditional retail models and reshaped the retail landscape. Bezos's relentless focus on innovation and customer satisfaction has driven Amazon's success and cemented its position as a dominant player in the digital economy. This chapter examines the impact of Amazon on global commerce and consumer behavior.

Jack Ma, the co-founder of Alibaba, has also been a key player in the digital economy. Alibaba's e-commerce platforms, such as Taobao and Tmall, have transformed the way businesses and consumers interact in China and beyond. Ma's vision of a connected and inclusive digital marketplace has driven Alibaba's success and positioned it as a global leader in e-commerce. This chapter explores the impact of Alibaba on the digital economy and the broader implications for global commerce.

Other billionaires, such as Elon Musk, have also ventured into the digital economy through initiatives like PayPal. Musk's vision of a cashless society and his innovative approach to digital payments have driven the adoption of online payment solutions and reshaped the financial landscape. This chapter examines the impact of digital payment solutions on global commerce and the transformative potential of the digital economy.

As we explore the digital economy and e-commerce, it becomes evident that billionaires play a crucial role in driving innovation and shaping the future of global commerce. Their ventures have transformed the way we conduct business and interact with the marketplace, creating new opportunities and challenges. This chapter critically examines the benefits and challenges of the digital economy, highlighting the need for thoughtful regulation and inclusive approaches to ensure that its potential is realized for the greater good.

15

Chapter 15: The Influence of Billionaire Sports Owners

Billionaire sports owners have a significant impact on the world of sports, shaping the future of teams, leagues, and the broader sports industry. Their investments and strategic decisions influence not only the performance of their teams but also the business of sports as a whole. This chapter explores the role of billionaire sports owners and the ways in which they are redefining the sports landscape.

Steve Ballmer, the former CEO of Microsoft and current owner of the Los Angeles Clippers, has brought a business-minded approach to sports ownership. His investment in the team and his commitment to building a new state-of-the-art arena reflect his vision of enhancing the fan experience and driving the team's success. Ballmer's approach to sports ownership highlights the importance of strategic investments and innovation in the business of sports.

Roman Abramovich, the owner of Chelsea Football Club, has also made a significant impact on the world of sports. His substantial financial investments in the club have enabled Chelsea to compete at the highest levels of European football, winning numerous domestic and international titles. Abramovich's ownership underscores the transformative potential of billionaire investments in elevating the performance and status of sports teams.

Other billionaire sports owners, such as Robert Kraft of the New England Patriots and Jerry Jones of the Dallas Cowboys, have also leveraged their wealth to build successful and iconic sports franchises. Their strategic decisions, investments in infrastructure, and focus on brand development have driven the success of their teams and reshaped the sports industry. This chapter examines the impact of billionaire sports owners on team performance, fan engagement, and the broader sports landscape.

As we explore the influence of billionaire sports owners, it becomes clear that their investments and strategic decisions have far-reaching implications for the business of sports. Their ability to drive innovation, enhance the fan experience, and build successful teams underscores the importance of visionary leadership in the sports industry. This chapter critically examines the benefits and challenges of billionaire sports ownership, highlighting the need for thoughtful approaches to ensure that the interests of fans, players, and communities are balanced.

16

Chapter 16: The Intersection of Wealth and Politics

The intersection of wealth and politics is a complex and often contentious issue. Billionaires, through their financial resources and influence, have the ability to shape political outcomes and drive policy changes. This chapter explores the role of billionaires in politics and the impact of their involvement on democratic processes and governance.

Michael Bloomberg, the former mayor of New York City and founder of Bloomberg LP, has been a prominent figure in the intersection of wealth and politics. His substantial financial contributions to political campaigns and advocacy for issues such as gun control and climate change have made him a powerful political player. Bloomberg's involvement in politics highlights the potential for billionaires to drive policy changes and influence public discourse.

Charles Koch, through his network of political organizations and think tanks, has also had a significant impact on American politics. The Koch network's strategic investments in political campaigns, lobbying efforts, and policy advocacy have shaped public policy on issues such as taxation, regulation, and healthcare. Koch's approach to political involvement underscores the potential for wealth to influence governance and policy outcomes.

Other billionaires, such as George Soros and Sheldon Adelson, have also leveraged their wealth to support political candidates and causes aligned with their values. Soros's Open Society Foundations and Adelson's substantial donations to political campaigns reflect their commitment to influencing political outcomes. This chapter examines the impact of their political involvement and the broader implications for democratic processes.

As we explore the intersection of wealth and politics, it becomes evident that billionaires play a significant role in shaping political outcomes and driving policy changes. Their financial resources and strategic investments have the potential to influence public discourse and governance. This chapter critically examines the benefits and challenges of billionaire involvement in politics, highlighting the need for transparency, accountability, and inclusive approaches to ensure that democratic processes are upheld.

17

Chapter 17: The Future of Billionaire Influence

As we look to the future, it is clear that billionaires will continue to play a significant role in shaping the world. Their influence extends beyond their financial wealth, encompassing technological innovation, philanthropy, political activism, and more. This chapter explores the future of billionaire influence and the potential paths that lie ahead.

One of the key factors that will shape the future of billionaire influence is the continued advancement of technology. Emerging fields such as artificial intelligence, biotechnology, and renewable energy hold immense potential for transformative change. Billionaires who invest in and drive innovation in these areas will have a significant impact on the direction of global progress. This chapter examines the potential for future technological advancements and the role of billionaires in shaping them.

Another important aspect of the future of billionaire influence is the evolving landscape of philanthropy. As new challenges and opportunities arise, billionaires will need to adapt their philanthropic strategies to address pressing global issues. This chapter explores the future of philanthropy, highlighting the importance of transparency, accountability, and inclusivity in ensuring that philanthropic efforts align with broader societal interests.

The political landscape is also likely to be shaped by billionaire influence. As billionaires continue to support political candidates and advocate for policy changes, their impact on governance and public policy will remain significant. This chapter examines the potential future of billionaire involvement in politics and the implications for democratic processes and governance.

Finally, the future of billionaire influence will be shaped by the actions and decisions of the billionaires themselves. As they navigate the complexities of their roles and responsibilities, their choices will have far-reaching consequences for society. This chapter explores the potential for positive change and the ethical considerations that will guide the future of billionaire influence.

Book Description

"Wealth of Nations Reimagined: How Billionaires Are Rewriting the Rules of Power" offers an in-depth exploration of the transformative influence wielded by modern billionaires. Through 17 insightful chapters, this book delves into the ways in which these powerful individuals are reshaping industries, driving technological advancements, and redefining the concept of wealth and power.

From the visionary leaders of the tech revolution to the influential philanthropists addressing global challenges, this book provides a comprehensive look at the diverse and far-reaching impact of billionaires. Each chapter examines a different facet of their influence, from their role in disrupting traditional industries to their involvement in global geopolitics and environmental advocacy.

With compelling stories and critical analyses, "Wealth of Nations Reimagined" offers readers a deeper understanding of the complexities and ethical considerations surrounding billionaire influence. It highlights the potential for positive change and the challenges that arise from concentrated power in the hands of a few.

As we navigate the ever-evolving landscape of the 21st century, this book serves as a thought-provoking guide to the ways in which billionaires are shaping our world. It encourages readers to reflect on the implications of their actions and the future of wealth, power, and societal progress.

www.ingramcontent.com/pod-product-compliance
Lightning Source LLC
LaVergne TN
LVHW020500080526
838202LV00057B/6062